SMOOTH-TALKING DOG

Phoneme Media
P.O. Box 411272
Los Angeles, CA 90041

First Edition, 2016

ISBN: 978-1-944700-08-9

This book is distributed by Publishers Group West

Cover art, design and typesetting by Jaya Nicely

Printed in the United States of America

Phoneme Media is a nonprofit media company dedicated
to promoting cross-cultural understanding, connecting people
and ideas through translated books and films.

http://phoneme.media

Curious books for curious people.

SMOOTH-TALKING DOG

DOG

Poems by
Roberto Castillo Udiarte

–

Translated from the Spanish
by Anthony Seidman

Introduction

Roberto Castillo Udiarte was born in 1951 in Tecate, Baja California, a smaller city that is now quickly turning into a suburb of Tijuana, due to TJ's urban sprawl. His family was not well off, but they were rich when it came to storytelling, and his parents were also avid readers who introduced him to classic authors like Mark Twain. As the city is located on the border, Castillo Udiarte heard English from a young age, and he fell in love with classic rock. His first translation of a poem was the lyrics to "Lady Jane" by The Rolling Stones. None of his classmates could understand what Jagger and others were singing about, and Castillo Udiarte became a poet and translator early in life. The majority of Tecate's younger residents hoped to find employment at the city's famous brewery, ideally as a chemical engineer. Castillo Udiarte soon realized that he wasn't the strongest at math and science, and some influential teachers encouraged him to pursue a degree in literature. After studying at the UNAM, in Mexico City, he returned to northern Mexico, settled in Tijuana, and spent decades as a university professor, running numerous workshops, editing journals, publishing chapbooks of local writers, and doing much to foment creation in the border region. The idea of a literature from the North was still a novel concept back then. In fact, many from Mexico City or Guadalajara would have considered the idea absurd.

There was a stubbornness and a bravery in Castillo Udiarte's stance as a creator. Until a decade or two ago, all supposedly serious art and writing was either produced or promoted in the Mexican capital. To a certain degree, Mexico remains a centralized country. The nation's capital is where many still go in order to "become" a writer or artist. (Think of Manhattan in 1940s or '50s United States.) For a long time, writers from Mexico City looked down on the North—and especially the border area— as regions where no literature of merit was produced. José Vasconcelos went so far as to say that culture in Mexico ceases wherever its inhabitants begin to prefer grilled meat. (Indeed, tacos varios, and tacos in tortillas de harina are the succulent meals preferred by most in Tijuana and Mexicali respectively.) Apart from completing his undergraduate degree in literature in the capital—where he took classes with Augusto Monterroso and other important writers—Castillo Udiarte was tenacious about writing from, and about, the border. It must have been a struggle at first, and one can imagine the snubbing he must have experienced from poets living in the capital, who would receive generous grants from the federal government, and who traveled to Paris, or wrote excessively exquisite verse. Castillo Udiarte opted to create a lexicon wherein the junkyards, red-light district dive bars, accordions, Spanglish and caló, and other daily realities from the border were mixed together in a vibrant impasto, creating a type of poetry never before imagined in Mexico, or in Spanish.

His stubbornness and bravery paid off. Castillo Udiarte, as a poet, teacher, editor, and publisher, has left an indelible mark on Mexican poetry. It is largely due to Castillo Udiarte that the literature from the North has become more recognized, more celebrated. Writers a generation or two younger than Castillo Udiarte benefitted much from his poetry and translations of contemporary North American poetry. Celebrated as the "Godfather of the Tijuana Counterculture," Castillo Udiarte helped validate the work of younger writers, such as Heriberto Yepez and Rafa Saavedra. Recently, Iberian scenesters, authors from the South, and others, have started to publish novels about the desert, about the border, and drug trafficking. I imagine this makes Castillo Udiarte chuckle. Even more absurd is the slow migration back North from writers who left Tijuana and Mexicali in order to live in Mexico City. Many spent years writing about

II

the border, but from a distance obscured by nostalgia and an absolute disconnect from the furious changes taking place.

The task of the translator is never easy, and the very sui generis poetry of Castillo Udiarte presents its own unique labyrinths. One of his most quoted and popular poems is "El perro labioso," the title poem of this volume. The poem, an open sequence of five parts, clearly situates itself within the tradition of urban poems, or novels, whose protagonist is the city itself. One thinks of Apollinaire's "Zone," of *Ulysses*, or Crane's "For The Marriage of Faustus and Helen," which dizzyingly reveals the paradise and hell of New York City. Castillo Udiarte opens with a sweeping panorama of the city; his technique relies on recreating the babble, the heteroglossia surging from diverse social classes. Rather than providing footnotes, I opted to recreate the numerous slang expressions, the tension between broken English and border region Spanish, quips, salacious double entendres, and brilliant images of pure poetic register. Other poems, such as his equally famous "The Magician of the Mirrors' Final Show," create a similar tableau of slang, northern Spanish, and anafora. My wildest versions and seemingly idiosyncratic choices received the poet's blessings. Clearly, Castillo Udiarte's own experience as a translator of Bukowski, Lamantia, Bill Knott, and others has helped him realize how challenging his own poetry is to render well into English.

Roberto and I spent many hours working at his kitchen table in Playas Tijuana, a fifteen-minute drive from the city's energetic downtown. I had the luxury of asking him directly about slang, tone, and allusions that I didn't grasp on my own. These sessions were accompanied by rich red wine from Baja California, classic rock and bebop on the stereo, and the usual walk to the corner Oxxo where I could buy some Indios and restock his cigarette supply. Ideal working conditions. While we worked, Roberto would recount past experiences with poet-friend Robert Jones, who died tragically at a young age, other writers from the region, adventures, and blazing nights in diverse places. Late one afternoon, we decided that a visit to his favorite bar, Dandy del Sur, would be a fitting way to wrap up a translation session. It was dusk by the time the taxi dropped us off. Inside, red leather booths, an old wooden bar top, and photos from past decades served as the backdrop for a crowd of mixed ages, couples, local artists, and writers. A jukebox played an unlikely set of songs: Juanga followed by Iggy Pop followed by Los Tucanes followed by Frank Sinatra. After a mezcal or two, he told me to accompany him outside for a quick Marlboro Red. The neon-illuminated sidewalk was teeming with young celebrants on their way to and from bars, dance clubs, steaming taco stands. No less than ten locals stopped to greet Roberto with a hug, while the young women would give a kiss to his beard. They were people who attended his workshops, aspiring writers, past students, and general acquaintances. I knew that this was the fondness he deserved. He was the one who never abandoned Tijuana or the border, who had given them a lasting body of work that celebrated them and their city. If I may riff on a declaration made by our greatest barbaric yawper: *The proof of a poet is that his metropolis absorbs him as affectionately as he has absorbed it.*

Now for the first time in English, we have a full volume of his lizard-tail blues, of his smooth-talking dog, of the streets and border-crossings that create an unforgettable poetry. Enjoy.

Anthony Seidman
Mexicali, September 2016

The Magician of the Mirrors' Final Show

La última función del mago de los espejos

Si usted vive en el valle de la felicidad
y hace ejercicio diariamente con su traje azul de iecipenis
mientras su esposa se acuesta con su mejor amigo,
pásele, pásele.

Si su esposo es un inútil
y usted es dama benefactora que ofrece dulces
y juguetes rotos a los niños pobres de La Obrera
cada seis de enero
y se siente feliz por su acción del año,
pásele, pásele.

Si usted es una señorita de nombres extraños
que paga al periódico por salir en las sociales
en busca de un junior o un apuesto ejecutivo
que la rescate del palacio de sus padres,
pásele, pásele.

Si usted es un ejecutivo,
un maniquí de oficina, sonrisa de fluoruro,
traje impecable de la sirs
y cree que la realidad es ser patrón de una empresa
y al llegar a casa golpea a su mujer e hijos,
pásele, pásele.

Si usted es una secretaria frustrada
que lee diariamente su horóscopo y las novelitas inéditas
de Vanidades y Cosmopolitan
y el cómo atrapar a su patrón en tres pasos
y una posición horizontal,
pásele, pásele.

The Magician of the Mirrors' Final Show

If you live in the valley of happiness
and work out every day, sporting your blue jumpsuit from JCPenney
while your wife two-times you with your best friend,
step right up, step right up.

If your husband's a ne'er-do-well,
yet you're a Lady of Benevolence who tosses candy
and busted toys to ghetto urchins
each holiday season,
and you feel fulfilled by this act of charity,
step right up, step right up.

If you're young, with an Anglo-sounding last name,
and you pay an exorbitant sum to splash
your photo on the society pages
to entrap some preppy or businessman
and get him to rescue you from your parents' mansion,
step right up, step right up.

If you're an executive,
an office mannequin with a fluoride-bleached smile,
wearing a dry-cleaned suit purchased from Sears,
and you believe that life is about being a company executive,
and upon getting home you beat your wife and children,
step right up, step right up.

If you're a frustrated secretary
who checks the daily horoscope, reads the new
inspirational speakers featured in supermarket aisle magazines:
How to Seduce Your Boss in Three Easy Steps
and One Horizontal Move,
step right up, step right up.

Si frecuenta los bares
repletos de gente sola
donde un trío canta las mismas canciones
desde hace veinticinco años,
o va a las cafeterías
a platicar sobre el destino de la nación
mientras ve pasar a las jóvenes empleadas
acariciadas por pantalones de mezclilla sergio caliente,
pásele, pásele.

Si usted es un hombre solo
o una mujer quedada
perdida entre la multitud silenciosa
y vive en un cuarto de hotel o un apartamento sin nada,
pásele, pásele.

Si usted hace cola para comprar tortillas o leche,
para entrar al cine, tomar el taxi o el camión
y se empuja para ganar un asiento
o se peleas en silencio,
pásele, pásele.

Si usted lee en el periódico
que una niña fue violada por un anciano,
que una anciana fue asaltada por un joven,
que la guerra estalló en todas partes,
que el precio del azúcar sigue subiendo
y no está conforme,
pásele, pásele.

Si eres un estudiante de futuro incierto
con los libros bajo el brazo
y un cuaderno de notas innecesarias,
pásale, pásale.

If you frequent the bars
filled with lonely folks,
where some trio has been twanging at the same songs
for the past twenty-five years,
or you sit in the coffee shop
in order to discuss the future of the nation,
while you stare at the young employees,
their flanks caressed by swap-meet denim,
step right up, step right up.

If you're a single man or
a jilted woman,
adrift in the silent crowds,
and you live in a furnished room or cheap apartment,
step right up, step right up.

If you stand in line to buy milk and tortillas,
to get into the movie theater, or take a taxi or the bus,
and you push your way to an empty seat,
or you struggle mutely,
step right up, step right up.

If you read in a newspaper
how a girl was raped by an old man,
or an old woman was mugged by some punk,
how war exploded everywhere,
and the cost of sugar shot up,
and you're against all of this,
step right up, step right up.

If you're a student facing a bleak future,
books and pages with useless notes
tucked under your arm,
step right up, step right up.

Si eres un profesor
que ve en cada alumna una posibilidad latente,
que impartes clases incomprensibles
para cubrir cincuenta minutos
y cobrar un sueldo insuficiente,
pásale, pásale.

Si eres un policía nocturno
resentido violador de cholitas
pásale, pásale.

Si eres un cholo
y la policía te persigue
por el hecho de ser cholo
y apareces diariamente en la nota roja
y tus pantalones, tu paliacate y tu virgencita tatuada
se desvanecen rápidamente,
pásale, pásale.

Si usted es un albañil
que desayuna gansitos con soda
y espera con ansiedad el día de pago
para comprar su Alarma y su Kalimán
y tomarse unos tequilitas en la Zona Norte,
pásale, pásale.

Si usted es una prostituta de la Zona Norte
donde las fuerzas vivas no se alcoholizan
y desde los quince años ha envejecido,
y bebe con obreros y gringos
y homosexuales vestidos de mujer,
pásale, pásale.

If you're a high school teacher
who glimpses some latent hopes beneath
the skirt of each student,
who teaches incomprehensible classes
in order to fill up fifty minutes
and cash a measly paycheck,
step right up, step right up.

If you're a cop, working the night beat,
resentful, raping the girls who live in the slums,
step right up, step right up.

If you're from the slums,
and the cops are after you
simply because you're from the slums,
and your mug is flashed on the daily news,
and your pants, your bandanna, and tattoo
of the Virgin are all fading quickly,
step right up, step right up.

If you're a construction worker
who starts his mornings with a candy bar and swig of soda,
and you anxiously wait for payday
to buy the tabloids, superhero comics,
and a few shots of tequila at some dive in the Zona Norte,
step right up, step right up.

If you're a streetwalker from the Zona Norte,
where the Rich and Beautiful never get drunk,
and you've been getting old since you were fifteen,
and you party with factory workers, gringos,
and homosexuals dolled up in drag,
step right up, step right up.

Si usted es un venderamosderosas,
limpiaventanillas, periodiquero,
tragafuegos, pordiosero que pide por dios
afuera de los bancos los bancos los bancos,
pásale, pásale.

Si usted es un sureño en busca de trabajo
que camina cabizbajo por calles con anuncios y ofertas
con un morral de colores chillantes y bolsillos rotos,
perseguido por ser ilegal,
encarcelado por ser ilegal,
condenado por ser ilegal,
pásale, pásale.

Si usted es un pepenador
que arrastra su mugre por las calles de la ciudad
o un borrachito o un loco urbano,
pásale, pásale.

Si usted lee lo que está aquí escrito
y se pregunta a dónde voy
qué trato de hacer o decir,
pásele, pásele,
dentro de unos instantes comenzará
la última función del mago de los espejos.

If you clean windshields, hawk flowers
or newspapers to cars idling at a red light,
or if you're a fire-eater, or a godforsaken beggar, yet begging
in the name of God outside the banks, the banks, the banks,
step right up, step right up.

If you're from down south, here just looking for a job,
and you trudge, downcast, through streets with billboards and bargains,
with a knapsack of garish colors and ripped pockets,
persecuted for being illegal,
jailed for being illegal,
condemned for being illegal,
step right up, step right up.

If you scavenge through bins,
and drag your trash down these city streets,
or if you're a drunkard or an urban lunatic,
step right up, step right up.

If you read what's written here
and ask where I'm headed with all this,
just what is it I'm trying to do or say, step right up, step right up,
we're just minutes from the curtains rising above
the Magician of The Mirrors' final show.

The Soul's Fingerprints

Huellas digitales del alma

En mi familia todos somos lagartos
de cáncer y acuario.
Antediluviano, el lagarto mayor,
acaba de morir cansado de la vida.
Otro, recostado sobre la piedra,
recuerda al que murió apedreado.
Una iguana tiene cataratas, la otra,
canas prematuras. Tías del valium
y tíos del alcohol. Un padre lagarto
que ríe y se preocupa constantemente,
una madre que se preocupa sin palabras
y una hermana del silencio.
Unas tías, las que se casaron tarde,
que niegan su cola de salamandra.
Un primo que juega con un aparato
que mira lo que nosotros no.
Unas verdiazules primas que están muy buenas
y una infinidad de lagartijas y sobrinillos
que juegan en las paredes de la casa
de los abuelos, esos sabios reptiles
que nada saben de máquinas ni poesía.

Yo, soy un lagarto onicófago
que escribe retratos de familia.

The Soul's Fingerprints

In my family we are all lizards born
under the signs of Cancer and Aquarius.
Antediluvian, the oldest lizard
has just died, weary of life.
Another one, stretched across a stone,
remembers the one who met his death by stoning.
One female iguana has cataracts, another,
hair gone prematurely gray. Aunts on Valium
and boozing uncles. A father lizard
who laughs, always worried,
a mother who worries yet says nothing,
and a silent sister.
Aunts who married late,
ashamed of their humble salamander tails.
A cousin who toys with a lens
gazing at something we can't see.
Some blue-green cousins with enthralling bodies,
and endless small lizards and little nephews
that frolic on the walls of their grandparents'
house, those wise reptiles
who know nothing about machines or poetry.

As for myself, I am a lizard who bites his nails
and writes family portraits.

Abuelo, ayer te conocí
por fotografía, en esa pose tradicional
de traje prestado, sombrero de palma
y mano derecha sobre un respaldo.
La falta de costumbre ante la cámara
delata tu sorprendida e inquieta sangre
aventurera.
Siempre te imaginé.
Ahora tu presencia llena el vacío
que ocupé con fantasías de pescador,
varillero, galán, marinero, sombras...

Grandfather, yesterday I met you
in a photograph; you, in that traditional pose
with borrowed suit, straw hat,
right hand on an armrest.
Unaccustomed to cameras, your
surprised and restless adventurer's blood
is betrayed.
I always imagined you.
Now your presence fills the emptiness
I peopled with the dreams of a fisherman,
a wandering salesman, handsome suitor, sailor, shadows...

Mi abuela, tres veces viuda,
dice que moriste hechizado como lagarto,
mas sé que, entrelíneas, algo esconde
cincuentaisiete años después,
algo que sólo ella y tú saben.

My grandmother, thrice a widow,
says you died spellbound like a lizard,
yet I know that between her words something
remains hidden, fifty-seven years later,
something only she and you know.

Anoche,
con la lluvia de diciembre,
entró a casa el recuerdo
de Felipe, uno de mis abuelos,
el del eterno jardín.

Y lo soñé
treinta años más joven,
sonriente, su cara picada por viruela,
su larga cola de lagarto.
Y en el sueño
me contó hazañas cardenistas,
de su llegada a la frontera,
la construcción de la presa
en Tijuana, su empleo de cantinero,
su primera mujer, el hijo adoptivo
y los interminables tequilas.

Esta mañana
amaneció una gotera azul
y no sé cómo explicarles a mis hijas
que ellas también son parte de mi abuelo.

Last night,
with the December rain,
the memory of Felipe
entered our house, one of my grandfathers,
the one from the eternal garden.

I dreamed of him
thirty years younger,
smiling, his face pockmarked,
and his long lizard's tail.
And in the dream
he told me of his exploits during the reign of Cardenas,
of his arrival at the border,
the construction of the Tijuana dam,
his job as a barman,
his first wife, his adopted son, and
the interminable shots of tequila.

A blue
leakage flooded this morning,
and I don't know how to explain to my daughters
that they too are part of my grandfather.

Mi abuelo,
el lagarto tropical,
engulle recuerdos y deseos
con toda la calma del mundo
mientras de su espalda tornasol
emergen dos puntitas emplumadas.

My grandfather,
the tropical lizard,
guzzles down memories and desires,
with all the calm in the world
while two feathers begin to sprout
from his iridescent back.

Ya no son exclusivas
de los Galápagos
la tristura, la paciencia
y la sabiduría,
tres cualidades
de la iguana del mar.
Mi abuela es un ejemplo.

Feeling blue, waiting,
and relying on prudence,
three qualities belonging
to the coastal iguana,
are no longer
exclusive to the Galapagos.
My grandmother is an example.

El tío Komodo
tiene fama de asesino
por el tamaño descomunal
de sus fauces y su cola.
Nada saben los humanos
de la fuerza de su amor
por toda nuestra familia.

Uncle Komodo,
because of the colossal size
of his fangs and tail,
is reputed to be a killer.
Humans know nothing
about of the strength of his love
for our entire family.

Mi tía cocodrila, falsa viuda,
gusta de asistir a funerales
en donde llora y llora a cambio
de un poco de café con alcohol
y unas ganas enormes de platicar.

My crocodile aunt, an aspiring widow,
delights in attending funerals;
she cries and cries in exchange
for a bit of coffee spiked with liquor
to slake an overwhelming need to chatter.

El mero 24 de diciembre,
día de su cumpleaños,
mi tío saurio,
el de abundante barba,
murió electrocutado
lejos de casa, lejos
de la piedra familiar.
La noche lluviosa
de su muerte,
una iguana desconocida llegó
con una hermosa iguanita,
igualita al tío saurio.

On the 24th of December,
his very birthday,
my saurian uncle,
the one with a long beard,
died from electric shock,
far from home, far
from the family stone.
On the rainy night
of his death,
a stranger iguana arrived
with a beautiful baby iguana
who looked just like my saurian uncle.

A mis padres les cambiaron
costas de arena caliente
por dunas y enormes rocas,
coloridas guacamayas y cocuyos
por águilas y verdes lagartos,
el calor de infancia tropical
por desierto y valle de encinos:
nuevos paisajes, nuevas maneras
de mirar la vida y las estrellas.

Ahora
desierto y valle son de ellos
por adopción voluntaria,
por derecho de amor.

They exchanged the coasts
and hot sand of my parents
for dunes and enormous rocks;
colorful macaws and fireflies
for eagles and green lizards;
the heat of a tropical childhood
for the desert and valley of oaks:
new landscapes, new ways
of looking at life and the stars.

Now
desert and valley are theirs
through their own will,
through their own loving right.

Macho lagarto,
uno de mis primos,
vive tras las rejas
de un zoológico extranjero
acusado de raptar
a una iguana en extinción
y de morder
a un biólogo respetable.

Tough lizard,
one of my cousins,
lives behind bars in a gringo zoo,
accused of having abducted
an iguana on the verge of extinction,
and of biting
a respectable biologist.

Mi camaleona
de piel verdosa
y ojos milenarios
me presume su encanto
mudando de color
a cada instante.

My lovely chameleon
of green skin
and ancient eyes,
she shows off her charm,
changing colors
every instant.

Desde cada roca miro
a mis cuatro iguanitas.

Sus colitas inquietas
dejan escritos ilegibles
sobre la ardiente arena
—un testimonio infantil—.

Aún nada saben
de su lugar en la historia
como continuadoras
de nuestra sangre reptil.

Upon each rock
I see my little iguanas.

Their restless tails
leave an illegible script
upon the burning sand,
testimonies of childhood.

They have yet to learn
of their place as successors
in the history
of our reptile's blood.

Zona Norte

Zona Norte

Lo que tú
nunca has querido decir
está escrito
en las paredes de los baños.

Zona Norte

What you
refused to say:
scribbled
above public urinals.

Apestoso a orines
y basura
el nómada urbano
canta en su rincón
ahí donde sus sueños de emperador
son realidad esta noche
y los perros
admiran el brillo
de su corona de cristal.

Stinking of piss
and litter
the urban nomad
sings from his corner, there,
where his dreams of being an emperor
take on flesh tonight,
and the stray dogs
admire the sparkle
of his glass crown.

El anciano
arrastra los pies descalzos
sobre tierra y vidrio.

Ha olvidado su nombre,
edad, familia...
Sólo le quedan
el orgullo de vivir
y una botella de alcohol.

The ancient man
drags his feet
across dirt and glass shards.

He's forgotten his name,
age, family...
The only thing he has left:
pride in being alive
and small bottle of liquor.

Estas manos que ves
empequeñeciendo
la botella de tequila
me defendieron de la muerte
una noche sin luna.

Sin embargo
estas manos enormes
estuvieron en 33 combates
y todos los perdí.

These very hands you see
making this tequila bottle
seem so tiny
defended me from Death herself
one moonless night.

However,
these enormous hands
were in 33 fights
and lost every one.

Cada fin de semana
cambia de nombre, lugar.
Desde los quince años
envejece
y en la calle no la reconoces,
es la mujer del vestido azul
a quien, una noche de invierno,
olvidaste pagar.

Each weekend
she changes her name, corner.
Since the age of fifteen
she has grown old
and you don't recognize her now on the street;
she's that woman in the blue dress
whom, one winter night,
you forgot to pay.

Entre cerveza y cerveza
la mujer baila
con hombres de sudor
y mal aliento.

(La música norteña
se arrastra
bajo las mesas
y sale por la cortina
que lucha por ser puerta).

Un enano, enorme resentido,
se acerca a la mujer
y le estrella una botella.

Between swigging beers
the woman dances;
the men sweat and pant
their rancid breath.

(The norteño ballad
drags itself under the tables
and scatters through the curtain
that struggles to be a door.)

A midget with an oversized grudge
approaches the woman,
shatters a bottle against her.

Pedir otra cerveza,
escuchar al ciego en el piano
y su compañera—cincuentona—
que canta un bolero sin nombre.

El mapa de sus vidas,
sombra de llanto y vidrio,
nubes trenzadas
a las patas de un piano
de teclas amarillas, negras,
desafinadas,
y en las pista,
una pareja de ancianos baila
y recupera algo que no veo.

To ask for another beer,
or listen to the blind man playing the piano,
as well as his fifty-something singer
belting out a nameless bolero.

The map of their lives,
umbrage of sobbing and glass shards,
clouds braided to the legs of a piano with
black and yellow keys
out of tune,
while on the dance floor
an elderly couple dances,
reliving something I can't make out.

Como siempre
cuando caiga
la última botella
caerán todas la máscaras.

As always,
when the last bottle falls
so shall
all of the masks.

A Soul's Cartography

Cartografía del alma

Diseminados por ríos, bosques,
pueblos, ciudades, zoológicos,
incluso cantinas del desierto,
es posible encontrar reptiles
contando historias extrañas
de raros peces que fueron,
de aves que serán...

A Soul's Cartography

Spread throughout rivers, forests,
towns, cities, zoos, and
even desert cantinas,
it's possible to find reptiles
telling strange stories
of odd fish that once were,
and of birds that have yet to be...

Esas huellas legibles
que dejan nuestras colas
en el polvo caliente
son cartografías del alma.
Ahí leemos alegría, tristura,
el amor y el desamor
de nuestro paso por la tierra.

Those legible traces
that our tails leave
in the hot dust
are soul maps.
From them we discover joy, feeling blue,
love and lovelessness,
and our voyage across the earth.

Varios cambios de piel
ha sufrido mi vida.
Cada mudanza
una cicatriz de amor,
un dolor de ausencia
que perdura bajo la piel.

My life has suffered
several changes of skin.
Each new change:
a love-scar,
an ache of absence
enduring beneath the skin.

Puedo perder un amor,
el rumbo o una batalla,
incluso una parte de mi cuerpo,
mi sangre antediluviana
me concede la supervivencia.

I can lose a lover,
my footing, or a battle,
even a body part...
for my antediluvian blood
ensures my survival.

A veces,
en mis sueños bajo el sol,
revivo mi estadio de agallas,
ojos sin párpados y aletas,
y al despertar, un sabor a sal
permanece en mi lengua
acostumbrada a las hormigas,
mariposas y saltamontes.

At times,
dreaming beneath the sun,
I relive my previous state: gills,
lidless eyes and fins;
upon awakening, a taste of salt
remains on this tongue
so accustomed to ants,
butterflies, and grasshoppers.

Desde esta roca ancestral
entro al paisaje en movimiento.

¿Soy acaso la imagen
que el saurio primigenio
imagino alguna vez
sobre esta misma roca?

From this ancestral rock
I enter the landscape, full of movement.

Am I perhaps the image
some primeval reptile
dreamt while perched
upon this very rock?

A veces me integro al paisaje
para no desentonar.
Otras,
para otorgarle movimiento.

Sometimes I hunker into the scenery
to blend;
other times,
to grant it movement.

En noches de ardiente verano,
mientras mis lagartas duermen,
pienso en los peligros de la piedra,
en la muerte emplumada del aire
y en la serpiente,
prima distante sin memoria,
que ataca con humana frialdad.

Para ellas tenemos tres armas:
astucia, agilidad y la unión
de los reptiles.

On sweltering summer nights,
while my lizards sleep,
I ponder the danger of stones,
feathered death plummeting from the air,
and the snake,
that distant cousin who has no memory,
and attacks with human cold-bloodedness.

Against them, I wield three weapons:
cunning, quickness, and reliance
on the unity of reptiles.

La inmovilidad
es otra táctica del lagarto.
Es aparente.
Sólo los reptiles percibimos
el movimiento perpetuo de la sangre.

Stillness
is another lizard strategy.
It's apparent.
Only we reptiles perceive
the perpetual movement of blood.

Cada escama de mi piel
es una medalla tornasol
obtenida en mis batallas
contra el abandono,
la tristura
y las garras acechantes
de la muerte emplumada.

Each hardened scale on my skin,
a sunflower-like medal
won during my battles
against abandonment,
feeling blue,
and the stalking claws
of feathered death.

Vivo constantemente en la frontera
que une las olas del mar y la tierra
—paso intermedio entre el pez y el ave—,
entre la vida y la muerte, por eso,
una condición para sobrevivir
es ser eterno reptil en duermevela.

I always live on the border
where ocean waves fuse with land—
an intermediate step between fish and bird—
between life and death, thus,
one condition for surviving:
be a reptile forever dozing.

Soy corteza de roca,
pedazo de paisaje
a veces en reposo.

Soy corteza vegetal,
pedacito de cactus
que emerge en silencio.

También soy sangre fría
en busca de un sentido
al universo reptil.

I am the crust of a rock,
a piece of the landscape,
sometimes at rest.

I am the crust of vegetation,
a small piece of cactus
that emerges in silence.

I am also cold blood
in search of the meaning
to the universal reptile.

Otorgo a los míos
la sangre alerta,
la experiencia vivaz
ante el enemigo que repta
y el peligro emplumado,
la posibilidad del mimetismo,
el placer de la inmovilidad
y la eficacia del movimiento.

To my beloveds, I leave behind:
blood always on alert,
the electrifying experience of sighting
the stalking enemy or
the feathered threat,
as well as the advantages of mimicry,
the pleasure in keeping still,
and the effectiveness
of flitting.

Lizard-Tail Blues

Reptilario

Su frenesí candente
de espiral infinita
muere, revive
—blues cola de lagarto—
del jukebox a nosotros
(al interior infierno
que lo rumia y regresa)
de la angustia a la angustia
    Francisco Morales

1

Inútil
que pretenda ignorar
al lagarto
tarde o temprano llega
sin tocar siquiera
la puerta.

2

Con el menor ruido
se arrastra
y repta
por escalones
la tristeza
subterránea.

Reptiliary

Its red-hot frenzy
of an infinite spiral
dies, is reborn—
lizard-tail blues—
from the jukebox for us
(into the infernal interior
which chews it, returns it)
from one anguish to another
    Francisco Morales

1

No use
trying to ignore
the lizard;
sooner or later it'll
arrive without even
knocking on the door.

2

With barely a sound,
dragging itself and
crawling up
the steps:
subterranean
sadness.

3

Con piel azul
cola verdosa y negra
se acerca
lentamente
se yergue en sus dos patas
traseras
y se asoma a mis ojos
me reconoce
me reconozco:
blues cola de lagarto.

3

With azure skin,
greenish black tail,
it slowly
approaches,
sits up on two hind
paws and peers
into my eyes;
it recognizes me,
I recognize myself:
lizard-tail blues.

Bluesecito

Hace varios días
que mi corazón
tiene mucho que ver
con una peluquería,
la botica cerrada
y el estacionamiento vacío.

Lil' Blues

For several days
my heart has shared
much in common with
a barbershop,
the shuttered drugstore,
and empty parking lot.

5:30 p.m.

Platos sucios,
servilletas amarillas,
cigarrillos, ceniceros nácar,
una fruta apenas mordida,
el ratón en la trampa,
el eco de una risa en el rincón
y la tibieza de las sillas:
ruinas cotidianas.

5:30 p.m.

Dirty plates,
yellow napkins,
cigarettes, mother-of-pearl ashtrays,
a once-bitten fruit,
the mouse caught in a trap,
echo of laughter in the corner,
and the slight warmth of chairs:
daily ruins.

La puerta del martes

Esta mañana,
al abrir la puerta del martes,
un perro amarillo agoniza
bajo el invierno.
Sus ojos
        miran algo que no comprendo,
algo
    que tiene que ver con diciembre
no con la tibieza de mi café.

Soy su última visión:
ante él me arrodillo.

Tuesday's Door

This morning
upon opening the door to Tuesday,
a yellow dog suffers the throes
of a winter death.
His eyes
            gaze at something I can't comprehend,
something
            that has to do with December
and not the tepidness of my coffee.

I am his last vision:
and before him, I kneel.

Tango

Mañanas
de café frío,
calcetines sin par,
pantalones sucios
de grasa y lodo;
mañanas de oscuridad de cartera.

Noches
de cerveza caliente,
colillas, tiendas cerradas
y del libro que no encuentro;
noches
en las que el enfado,
en silencio,
se sienta a mi mesa
en espera del amanecer.

Tango

Mornings,
cold coffee,
matchless socks,
pants filthy
with grease and mud;
mornings with a dark wallet.

Nights,
warm beer,
cigarette butts, closed shops,
and the book I can't find;
nights
in which boredom
silently
sits on my table
and awaits dawn.

Almanaque

Hay días
en que el coraje
me rasga atrozmente
las axilas
y empequeñece mi estómago.

Días
en que la rutina
hace nuevamente
de las suyas
mientras el peine,
triunfante,
acumula mis cabellos.

Calendar

There are days
when a rage
viciously tears at
my armpits
and crushes my stomach.

Days
when the routine
plays itself out
while my comb
triumphantly
accumulates more of my hair.

Ropa sucia

Claxon de carros,
la falta de agua,
tardanza de quincenas,
cateos domiciliarios,
encarcelamientos y
baladas sentimentalonas,
la libertad condicional
y la muerte de los amigos,
son algunas de las cosas
que me disgustan,
son
ese algodón
emergiendo entre las costuras
de la muñeca de trapo
que algunos llaman realidad.

Dirty Laundry

Cars honking,
the water shut off,
paychecks delayed,
search warrants,
imprisonment and
sappy ballads,
freedom on parole,
and friends' deaths
are some of the things
I loathe:
they're
that cotton stuffing
coming out from the seams
of a ragdoll
some call reality.

Smooth-Talking Dog

El perro labioso

1

Damas y caballeros,
welcom tu Tijuana,
el lugar más mítico del mundo,
donde las lenguas se aman y se unen
en el aló, el oquei, el babai y el verbo tu bi;

donde existe la zona libre,
la fayuca y los regalitos
pal patrón, la secretaria,
la comadre cachonda, la esposa
y los hijos inaguantables;

donde los pizzeros en moto,
los patrulleros, los taxis,
los narcojuniors, sus compas
y las señoras con placas de California,
no respetan semáforos ni altos;

amigas y amigos,
bienvenidos a Tijuana,
la ciudad más lejana del centralismo,
donde sí saben los clamatos y el parizón,
donde florecen los yonkes y los mofleros;

donde las cuadras son espacios
pa'boticas, licorerías, casa de cambio,
taquerías, Oxxos al por mayor
y restaurantes de mariscos;

donde la comida regional
son la carne asada y la cerveza,
la langosta y los fish tacos,
la ensalada císars, la pizza
y la comida china dominguera;

Smooth-Talking Dog

1

Ladies and Gentlemen,
bienvenidos a Tijuana,
the most mythical place on the face of the earth,
where two tongues make-out and meld,
and the locals speak *He-loh, oh-kaye,* and the verb *tu bi;*

where the duty free zone exists,
the black-market and lil' gifts
for the boss-man, the secretary,
the thick and juicy girlfriend, the wife
and the unbearable children;

where the pizza-men astride speeding scooters,
the patrol cars, the taxis,
spoiled narco-brats, their buddies,
and the ladies bearing California license plates
respect neither traffic lights or stop signs;

friends, both guys and gals,
welcome to Tijuana,
the city flung the furthest from the nation's capital,
where the best Clamatos are mixed, wildest block-parties thrown,
where junkyards and muffler shops sprout like flowers;

where the urban blocks are spaces
for pharmacies, liquor stores, money exchangers,
taco shacks, Oxxos everywhere,
and seafood joints;

where the regional cuisine
consists of broiled beef and beer,
lobster and fish tacos,
Cesar salads, pizza,
and takeout Chinese every Sunday;

bienvenidos a Tijuas,
el lugar de la arquitectura emergente,
de las mujeres que son casa,
muelas que son consultorios
y sombreros que son restaurantes;

el maravillosos espacio
donde las llantas usadas
se transforman en escalones,
en columpios, muros de contención,
macetas y suelas pa'huaraches;

donde el Comité de Turismo
cree que lo único importante
son las torres de la Chapu,
la bola del Cecut, la Plaza Río,
el Jai Alai, la Revo y el Minarete.

Damas y caballeros,
bienvenidos a Tiyei,
donde cholos, surfos y panquillos,
narcos, sicarios y judiciales,
hacen del ocio su negocio;

donde políticos y empresarios,
maquiladores y aduaneros,
comerciantes y casacambistas,
loteros y policías,
son los verdaderos ilegales;

donde la polka se vuelve cumbia,
el norteño se hace tecno,
los mofleros son escultores,
los pintores son grafiteros
y la cultura está en la Zona Norte;

welcome to Tijuana,
the place for emerging trends in architecture:
woman-shaped houses,
tooth-shaped dentists' offices,
sombrero-shaped restaurants;

the marvelous space
where used tires
are transformed into staircases,
swings, retention walls,
flower pots and soles for leather sandals;

where the Department of Tourism
finds only the following places to be important:
the Chapu skyscrapers, the ball-shaped Cecut building,
the Plaza Rio shopping center, the Jai Alai,
the clubs on La Revolución and the Minaret.

Ladies and Gentlemen,
bienvenidos to TJ,
where homies, surfers, and punks,
narcos, cut-throats, and detectives
make a vacation of their vocation.

where politicians and investors,
factory bosses and customs agents,
businessmen and money changers,
lottery ticket hawkers and policemen
are the true illegals;

where the polka beat becomes a cumbia,
norteño become techno music,
muffler men are sculptors,
painters are taggers,
and culture is found in the Zona Norte;

señores y señoritas,
bienvenidos a Tijuana,
donde se unen compiúres y corazones,
las tecnologías nuevas con las viejas
y los burros se rayaron;

el zoológico nortense
donde coyotes y polleros,
la chiva, el perico y el gallo,
Los Tigres y Los Tucanes,
son animales millonarios;

donde la hermosísima Calafia,
reina legendaria de California,
primero fue convertida en vino
y ahora, triste y olvidada,
sólo es un transporte público;

welcom tu Tijuana,
la ciudad de las luces y hogar de Juan Soldado,
el santo de los migrantes,
amo y señor de los milagritos;

la casa de la leche Jersey,
del niño con gorrita beisbolera
y sonrisa fortificante,
que suple a las madres
en alimentación infantil;

donde hacer cola en la línea
pa' ir p'al otro lado de compras
se vuelve un martirio de dos horas
o una agria eternidad de claxon
y agandalles por ganar un espacio;

guys and gals,
welcome to Tijuana,
where computers and hearts are assembled,
old technologies with the new,
and zebra stripes are spray-painted on donkeys;

the northern melting pot
where coyotes and their gofers,
the dragon, the white horse, and Mary Jane,
Los Tigres and Los Tucanes
are all millionaire species;

where Calafia,
legendary queen of California,
was first transformed into wine
and now, sad and abandoned,
is just a public transportation line;

welcum to Tijuana,
the city of lights,
the home of Juan Soldado,
the patron saint of immigrants,
Master and Lord of Small Miracles;

the Jersey milk company with
their trademark boy in a baseball cap
and enriched smile,
which replaces mothers
as a source of infant nutrition;

where waiting in line
in order to cross the border and go shopping
becomes a two hour martyrdom
or a bitter eternity of honking horns
and rear-ending just to get ahead;

welcom tu Tijuana,
tierra prometida de migrantes,
nacionales y extranjeros,
donde vale mucho la vida
y la muerte es un negocio;

donde héroes desconocidos
adornan avenidas con glorietas;
donde da igual tener a Lincoln,
Cuauhtémoc, San Rocket o
una escultura incomprensible;

bienvenidos a Tijuana,
la calle, la frase inesperada,
la cachondez y el sistema binario,
el cruce fronterizo y el albur,
el irse pa'lla' y venirse pacá.

welcom tu Tijuana
promised land for migrants,
natives, and foreigners,
where life costs a great deal
and death is a big business;

where unknown heroes
rise above the avenues and roundabouts;
where it doesn't make a difference if it's a statue of Lincoln,
Cuauhtemoc or San Rocket, or
just some jumble of a sculpture;

welcome to Tijuana,
the street, the unexpected quip,
horniness and the binary system,
the border crossing and the double entendre,
the goin' over there and the happy endin' here.

2

Frente a laterenidad de la semana
y el ansia comeuñas del trabajo
está el horizonte de reven entresemanero,
el tirar barra con los compitas de la vida,
el arribo de los seises y el tequilotrón,
los colores del acordión y el tsssshhhh del bote,
la obligada conversación acerca de las morritas,
amores frustrados, amores dulces, amores porvenir,
el cómo no, el bien acá, el pistito de cariño,
el recordar frases que son literatura,
metáforas de los griegos y Omar Khayam,
Josealfredo o la sabiduría de Daniel Santos,
y arrimarse a la mesa questá a tu lado
con el pretexto de un cigarro o el cerillito,
de abrir amistades en corazones ajenos,
de platicar del clima, el fútbol, las votaciones,
de la inseguridad social ante unos ojos bonitos
y luego intercambiar deseos y números telefónicos,
reír con la risa guardada durante semanas,
iniciar lo que puede ser una amistá de kilates
porque del patriarca Noé hasta nosotros
una misma copa de cristal…¡salucita!

2

Ahead of the workweek's eternity
and the nail-biting anxiety at work,
a weekend-long party's on the horizon,
slamming down some brewskies with lifelong buddies,
picking up six-packs and tequila,
the accordion's colors and the *shlack!* of a beer cracking open,
the much-needed conversations about women,
failed loves, sweet loves, future loves,
the hell yeah, the very cool, the down the hatch,
remembering phrases from literature,
metaphors from the Greeks and Omar Khayam,
Josealfredo or the wisdom of Daniel Santos,
ask those at the table nearby for a smoke or match,
open friendships in hearts already taken,
talk about the weather, soccer, the elections,
about such sappy feelings when staring into some lovely eyes,
and then exchanging best wishes, phone numbers,
laughing with all the laughter pent up during the week,
starting what could be a golden friendship
because this shot goes for all of us,
from Noah's time till now...Cheers!

3

Tras el carrillón del día y el acelere mental,
cuando el cuerpo es casi ya un arnero
y la sangre endiablada se te alenta,
cuando se pega el flotador de lo cotidiano,
y la arritmia te desclocha el corazón,
es hora de abrir las puertas del lugar
en busca de calor y palabras de cura,
momento de la heladez de las caguas,
el sindicato de compas de tabaco y alcohol,
la amistad de plantígrados y hienas,
de darle sentido a la vida y a la muerte,
de aventar carcajadas al cielito lino
al son de la guitarra que guitarrea.

De pronto La Belle, epifanía entre el argüende,
calladita con el silencio de la roca y la flor,
llega y abre el mar con una sonrisa.
(El deseo te da rasquera en el alma. ¡Órale pues!)
Felino en acecho, lento pero seguro, atacas.
Sueltas la totacha de la corte y la conquista,
el sabroso guaguaguá en el oído femenino,
y mordisqueas con besos de toloache
al cuellito de la noche que aún es joven,
y cais al embrujo, a la morralla de las caricias,
las pasiones bonitas y al anchor de la felicidad.

Santificado, desmañanado e insomne de amor,
caminas por las calles del día, todo lurio,
con el sabor de su cuerpo en tu boca.

After the haste of the workday and its mental overdrive,
when the body has become a sieve,
and devilish blood urges you on,
when the daily routine sticks to you like a float,
and arrhythmia untwists your heart,
and it's time to open the doors
in search of warmth and soothing words,
the moment for ice-cold forties of beer,
the workers' union, allies of nicotine and alcohol,
the friendship between plantigrade males and hyenas,
in order to make some sense of life and death,
to laugh wildly at Cielito Lindo
keeping time to the guitar that guitars away.

And suddenly La Belle, an epiphany among the ruckus,
with the silence of the stone and flower,
she arrives and opens the sea with a smile.
(And lust lights up your soul, Hell yeah!)
Feline, stalking slowly, certain, you attack.
You recite some courtly slang and seduce her,
that delectable dog's panting in the feminine ear,
and you nibble the neck of the still-young night
with kisses which cause swooning like a toloache brew,
you succumb to the bewitchment, to the flitting of caresses,
to lovely passion, swollen with joy.

Sanctified, brimming over with love, and sleeplessness,
you roam the streets of day, crazed,
savoring the taste of her body on your tongue.

4

Pues sí, salir de la cantina más distante,
sin un quinto y la brújula voltiada,
sin cigarros y las llaves que no encuentras,
agarrar camino con el estéreo a todo volumen,
pensando en tu mujer bajo las cobijas,
dormida y ausente a tu briago corazón:
y ai vas, como loquito,
esquivando fantasmas y policías,
presto pa' llegar pronto a casa
lo más pronto posible; y luego llegar
y no atinarle a la cerradura que se mueve,
y subir la escalera con el menor ruido,
maldesvestirse y arrimarte como si nada,
tirando verbos, historias y evangelios,
dando besitos de cariño, besitos deadeveras,
y tu morrita, con toda la paciencia del mundo,
porque te ama, porque te conoce, porque se conoce,
voltea con la somnolienta mirada de una reina
y te dice: ¡ya duérmete, cabrón!

4

Yes siree, to exit the furthest cantina,
without a dime, your sense of direction spinning,
without cigarettes, your keys somewhere,
you set off on the road, with the stereo blasting,
thinking of your lil' lady beneath the blankets,
asleep already, absent from your drunken heart;
and there you go, like a nutcase,
avoiding ghosts and cop cars,
aching to get home as quickly as
possible; and then to arrive,
and to unclick the lock without making a squeak,
and to go up the stairs without creaking any steps,
to toss your clothes to one side and snuggle up
like nothing happened, toss out a few words, stories, gospels,
giving sweet kisses, authentic kisses,
and your main squeeze, who possesses all the patience
of the world only because she loves you, knows you, knows
herself, rolls over, facing you with a regal and
sleepy gaze, saying: Go to sleep, fucker!

5

A pesar de los pleitos entre los intolerantes de la palabra,
del friazo en las manos de quienes dicen gobernarnos,
gracias a la vida, digo, bien envinado esta noche de invierno;
gracias a la fámili, a los compas y las compitas deste planeta,
porque en nuestras venas siguen latiendo sangre y corazón,
sembrando un bonche de esperanza en la oscuridá del mundo
que nos pertenece "por derecho de amor", como dice Josemilio,
y orgullosamente tecatero presumo el calorcito de la vida,
la comparto humanamente con el deseo más buenonda,
como aquella noche otoñal cuando me dijo dios: "yo soy tu compa".

5

Despite the fighting between those intolerant of words,
despite the icy hands of those who supposedly govern,
I give thanks to life, warm with wine on this winter night;
thanks to the folks at home, the guys and gals who keep things real,
because blood and heart continue beating in our veins,
sowing a cluster of hope into the world's darkness,
the world which belongs to us by dint of love, like Josemilio sings,
and proudly from Tecate, for me life is warmth,
and I share it from one brother to another, with the best of intentions,
just as on that autumn night when God himself told me: I'm your bro.

We Live Several Lives At Once

Nuestras Vidas Son Otras

Eres la heroína de esta película
y una treintena de actores y actrices
se reparten ibretos y espacios
y voltean a las cámaras, mientras tú,
en silencio, paseas por el escenario
con la seguridad del discreto guionista.
No diriges a nadie, nadie te dirige
en esta película en blanco y negro
de la cual no sé el final,
y por eso me levanto de la butaca,
entro a escena por una esquina rota,
te busco en tus ojos
y encuentro toda la soledad del mundo
y la tristeza musical de Janis Joplin.
Aunque sé que nuestras vidas son otras,
quiero ser tu héroe de celuloide
aunque sea sólo por esta noche.

We Live Several Lives At Once

You're the heroine of this movie;
'round thirty actors and actresses
review their lines, go to their spots,
and turn to the cameras, while you
pass silently through the set, full
of confidence, like the scriptwriter.
You address no one, no one addresses you,
not in this black-and-white movie
whose ending remains a mystery to me,
and it's because of this
I get up from my seat,
enter the scene through a broken corner,
and look you in the eyes:
I discover the world's solitude,
the sad music of Janis Joplin.
Although I know we live several lives at once,
I wish to be your celluloid hero,
if only for tonight.

Te imagino detrás de un escritorio
o de un inútil salón de clases,
lejos de la familia del silencio,
y tal vez sepas de pronto
que no es fácil abandonarlos
porque el sentimiento de culpa
es una farsa difícil de jugar,
y tu madre seguramente
llorará su tragedia cotidiana
y tu padre, borracho otra vez,
se olvidará un poco más de ustedes,
y una culpa que es ajena
te joderá día tras día
y sabes
que sólo tienes dos salidas
porque nuestras vidas son otras.

I imagine you behind a desk,
or in some shabby classroom,
far from a family of silence,
and perhaps you find out too soon
that it's difficult to leave them behind,
because the feeling of guilt
is a farce that's hard to play,
and your mother will most likely
weep her daily tragedy,
and your father, drunk again,
will forget about you all a little more,
and someone else's guilt
will mess with you day after day,
and you know
you have only two ways out,
because we live several lives at once.

Veinte años hace de mi cabello largo,
los desteñidos livais y la música
de los Stones y Doors y tú,
entonces, apenas una niña
menor de diez años, delgadita, sonriente,
ojos negros y luminosos.
Nunca imaginé estar frente a ti
veinte años después, como hoy,
aún de livais, calvicie y barba,
hablándote de música, recuerdos,
reencuentros en la vida
y algunos poemas sin terminar
mientras tú, delgada y sonriente,
los mismos ojos brillantes,
me platicas tus visiones tecatenses
en aquellos años infantiles cuando yo,
tontamente feliz, me creía Morrison o Jagger.

Nuestras vidas son otras;
sin embargo esta noche, ante ti,
ya no creo ser Morrison ni Jagger
pero juego a que lo soy.

Twenty years ago,
I grew my hair long,
wore faded Levi's, carried my LPs
of The Stones, The Doors, and you,
barely ten, were a lithesome
and smiling girl
with black eyes that glistened.
I never imagined standing before you
twenty years later, like today,
still in my Levi's, with thinning hair,
bearded and dissipated
as any rock'n'roller,
speaking to you about
music, memories, chance
encounters in life,
and some poems without endings,
while you, lithesome and smiling,
with the same glisten in your gaze,
speak your childhood visions of Tecate,
during those years when I,
blissfully naïve,
thought of myself as Morrison or Jagger.

We live several lives at once;
but tonight, in front of you,
I no longer believe I'm Morrison or Jagger...
but I play at it like I am.

Frente al espejo
nuestros cuerpos reflejan
sus pequeñas guerras cotidianas.
No nos pertenecemos,
nuestras vidas son otras y
peleamos contra el destino
y deseamos, a veces,
la muerte de los seres que amamos
porque el amor es un ángel ilegal
que alisa su plumaje, casi siempre,
entre dos personas extrañas.

Before the mirror
our bodies reveal their
petty daily battles.
Our selves don't belong to us,
we live several lives at once;
we struggle against our fate,
and at times we wish
for the death of those we love,
because love is an outlaw angel
who, almost always,
smooths its feathers
between two perfect strangers.

Crows

Corvufobia

Porque la cuerva también llora.
Tomás Di Bella

Los hombres, en su finita maldad,
endiosaron a la inútil paloma,
al cordero silencioso
y a los peces que nunca cierran sus ojos;
en cambio inventaron la usura del hermano lobo
y el coyote, castigaron al grandioso bisonte
y la sigilosa serpiente sin párpados,
al alacrán del veneno de oro
y a las arañas de paciencia infinita;
a los pumas los desalmaron
junto con las ratas de ojos rojizos;
encarcelaron al zorro
y amarraron con grilletes al oso gentil,
al reno lo embozaron
al igual que al caballo y el venado de tercio pelo;
encarcelaron a los hermanos halcones,
cuervos, águilas y cóndores;
condenaron en libros al divino dragón de fuego,
el fálico unicornio, la sirena del bello canto,
al tiburón milenario y la ballena de lunas,
y mandaron al exilio toda bestia rebelde
al capricho del mandato, incluyendo los sueños,
los cantos, los deseos y al hombre mismo.

Crowphobia

Because the crow also weeps.
  Tomás Di Bella

Man, within the limits of his evil,
made the useless dove into a god,
as well as the silent lamb
and the fish with eyes never shut;
in exchange, he equated usury with brother wolf
and the coyote, punished the great bison
and the secretive serpent with no eyelids,
the scorpion with its golden venom,
and the spiders who possess infinite patience;
he slandered the pumas
alongside rats with reddish eyes;
he imprisoned the fox
and shackled the gentle bear;
he put reins on the horse,
as well as the velvety doe and the reindeer;
he caged the brother hawks,
crows, eagles, and condors;
in his books, he condemned the divine dragon of fire,
the phallic unicorn, the siren and her beautiful songs,
the ancient shark and the whale of a hundred moons,
and thus he banished each rebellious beast,
and uttered this mandate on a whim, casting out dreams,
singing, desire, even man himself.

El silencio del cuervo

Y no miento si digo
que Paul Eluard saltó de mi habitación
con alas de Ícaro y cuervo
por la ventana de esta ciudad.

Uberto Stabile

El silencio del cuervo
es una piedra negra en el cielo,
nube de lluvia que rompe el aire
sin hacer ruido, sin hacer viento;

navaja de obsidiana
que abre el corazón del cielo,
densa lluvia de sangre azabache,
ritual mudo para sanar el alma;

el silencio del cuervo
es una danza ausente de sonidos,
es un baile milenario sin historia,
es música carente de intenciones;

escritura silente del aire
que desaparece tan pronto aparece
y su intención no es permanecer
porque es tan fugaz como la vida;

el silencio del cuervo
así es, distante, ido, muy lejano,
aunque pueda resurgir su graznido
muy amoroso bajo la luz de la luna.

Silence of the Crow

And I am not lying if I say
Paul Eluard leapt from my room
with the wings of Icarus and the crow
through the window of this city.
  Uberto Stabile

The silence of the crow
is a black stone in the sky,
raincloud shattering the air
without stirring noise or wind;

obsidian knife
cutting open the sky's heart,
thick rainfall of jet black blood,
silent ritual for soul-healing;

the silence of the crow
is dancing rendered in silence,
an ancient dance without history,
is music without meaning;

silent scripture of the air
disappearing as soon as it appears,
it desires mutability
because it is as fleeting as life;

the silence of the crow
is just like that, distant, gone, far off,
although at any moment it might revive
an amorous cawing beneath the moonlight.

Cuervo de luz

As you know, the raven speaks in two voices, one harsh and strident, and the other,
which he uses now, a seductive bell-like croon which seems to come from the depths
of the sea, or out of the cave where the winds are born; it's an irresistible sound, one
of the loveliest sounds in the world.
Bill Reid

Soy el cuervo,
señor de la noche,
y nadie imagina mi canto
en el diario amanecer del mundo,
mi graznido amoroso, mi grito de vida.

Soy el cuervo,
amo de los cielos,
y en mis alas de ébano
cantan los vientos helados del norte
y en mi corvado pico yo guardo la luz.

Soy el cuervo,
plumaje de ónix,
ladrón de la luz de los dioses,
dador de toda la vida septentrional
a plantas, animales y parejas humanas.

Soy el cuervo,
dueño del cielo azulado,
y mi vuelo del silencio
augura los buenos mensajes
a los nativos de los territorios del sol.

Soy el cuervo,
sanador de almas,
curandero de las tristezas,
medicina natural de los corazones
que han perdido el rumbo en su trajinar.

Crow of Light

As you know, the raven speaks in two voices, one harsh and strident, and the other, which he uses now, a seductive bell-like croon which seems to come from the depths of the sea, or out of the cave where the winds are born; it's an irresistible sound, one of the loveliest sounds in the world.
    Bill Reid

I am the crow,
lord of the night
and nobody imagines my canticle
on each dawning of the world,
my amorous cawing, my cry of life.

I am the crow,
master of the heavens,
on my ebony wings
the icy northern winds sing,
and within my bent beak I hold the light.

I am the crow,
plumage of onyx,
thief of the light belonging to the gods,
giver of the northern life
to plants, animals and human couples.

I am the crow,
owner of the azure sky,
and my silent flight
is an augury of good tidings
to the natives of the sun's territory.

I am the crow,
healer of souls,
shaman against sadness,
natural medicine for the hearts
that have lost their way while rambling.

Soy el cuervo,
el amo del amor,
fiel a mi compañera de vuelo
durante el transcurso de toda la vida
y cuidador de los hijos emplumados.

Soy el cuervo,
constelación celestial,
nocturnal divinidad emplumada,
oscuridad repleta, granate oscurecido,
ave que limpia los caminos de la vida.

I am the crow,
the master of love,
loyal to my flight's companion
during a lifetime's course,
and the sentinel of feathered children.

I am the crow,
celestial constellation,
nocturnal feathered divinity,
flushed with darkness, dusky garnet,
bird that cleanses the roads of life.

Some of the translations first appeared in the following journals: *The Bitter Oleander, Huizache, San Diego Poetry Annual, Skidrow Penthouse,* and *World Literature Today.* Much gratitude.

Anthony Seidman is a poet and translator from Los Angeles. He began translating Mexican literature during the five years that he lived in Ciudad Juárez. His most recent book of poetry, *A Sleepless Man Sits Up in Bed,* appeared in 2016, and his most recent translation is J.M. Servín's memoir *For Love of the Dollar: A Portrait of the Artist as an Undocumented Immigrant.*